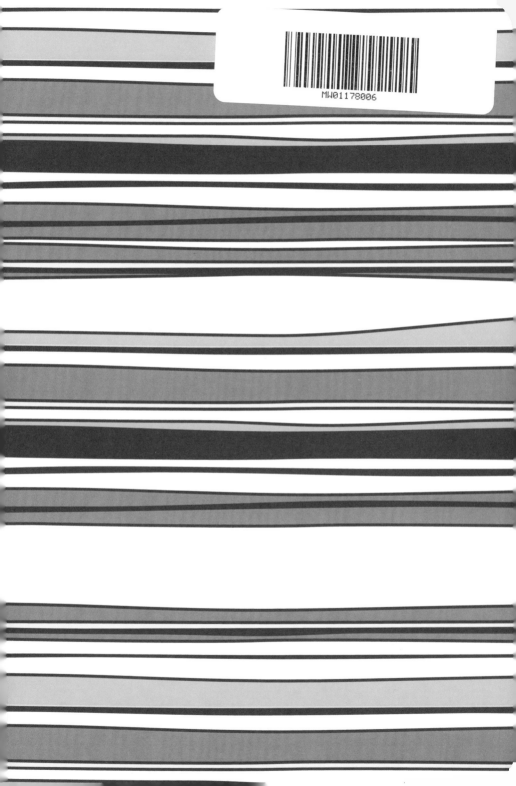

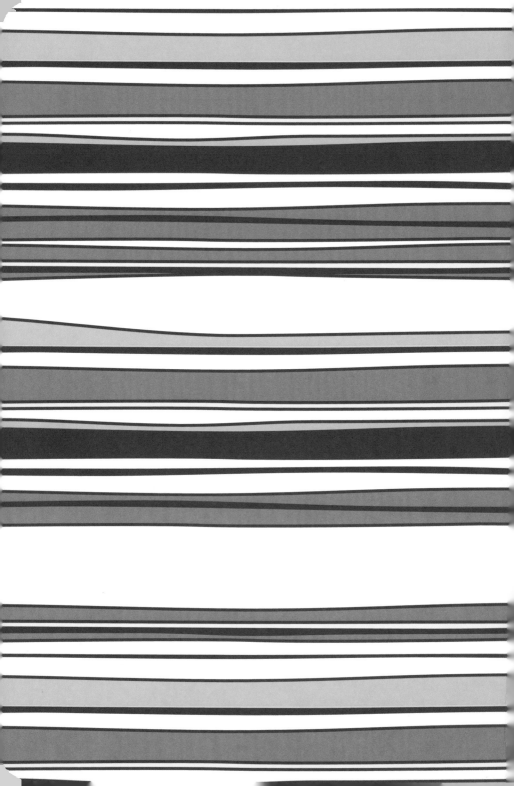

To: _____

From: _____

Date: _____

"For I know the plans I have for you," declares the LORD.

Jeremiah 29:11

Delight yourself in the Lord and He will
give you the desires of your heart.
Psalm 37:4

_____

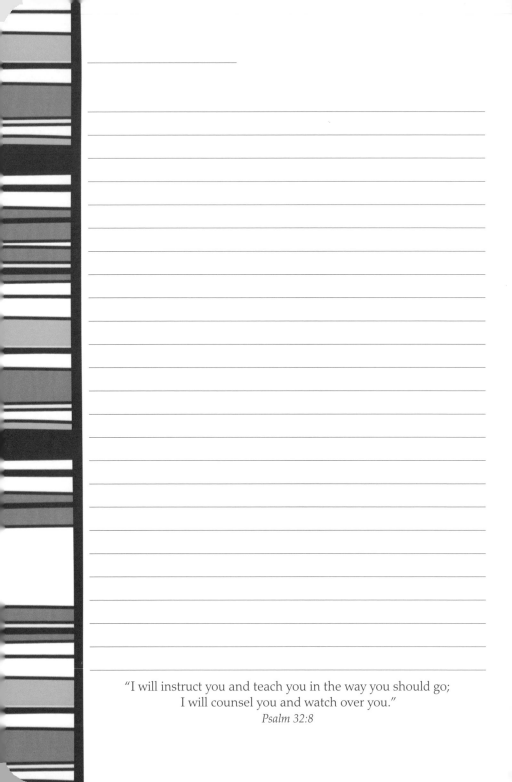

"I will instruct you and teach you in the way you should go;
I will counsel you and watch over you."
Psalm 32:8

Commit to the LORD whatever you do,
and your plans will succeed.
Proverbs 16:3

Search me, O God, and know my heart; test me and know
my anxious thoughts. See if there is any offensive way
in me, and lead me in the way everlasting.
Psalm 139:23-24

The eternal God is your refuge,
and underneath are the everlasting arms.
Deuteronomy 33:27

Those who hope in the LORD will renew their strength. They will
soar on wings like eagles; they will run and not grow weary,
they will walk and not be faint.

Isaiah 40:31

"I have come that they may have life, and have it to the full."
John 10:10

O LORD, You are my God; I will exalt You and praise Your name,
for in perfect faithfulness You have done marvelous things.

Isaiah 25:1

_____

_____

_____

_____

_____

_____

_____

_____

_____

_____

_____

_____

_____

_____

_____

_____

_____

_____

_____

_____

_____

_____

_____

_____

_____

_____

_____

"I know the plans I have for you," declares the Lord, "plans to prosper
you and not to harm you, plans to give you hope and a future."
Jeremiah 29:11

Shout for joy, O heavens; rejoice, O earth; burst into song,
O mountains! For the Lᴏʀᴅ comforts His people.
Isaiah 49:13

"Peace I leave with you; My peace I give you. Do not let your hearts be troubled and do not be afraid."

John 14:27

He who began a good work in you will carry it on
to completion until the day of Christ Jesus.
Philippians 1:6

We know that in all things God works for the good of those
who love Him, who have been called according to His purpose.
Romans 8:28

Blessed are those who walk in the light of Your presence,
O Lord. They rejoice in Your name all day long;
they exult in Your righteousness.
Psalm 89:15-16

God is able to make all grace abound to you, so that
in all things at all times, having all that you need,
you will abound in every good work.
2 Corinthians 9:8

_____

"The Lord bless you and keep you; the Lord make His face
shine upon you and be gracious to you; the Lord turn
His face toward you and give you peace."
Numbers 6:24-26

God has said, "Never will I leave you; never will I forsake you."
Hebrews 13:5

Every good and perfect gift is from above, coming down from
the Father of the heavenly lights, who does not
change like shifting shadows.

James 1:17

May the God of peace equip you with everything good for doing
His will, through Jesus Christ, to whom be glory for ever and ever.
Hebrews 13:20-21

The Lord is good, a refuge in times of trouble.
He cares for those who trust in Him.
Nahum 1:7

As the deer pants for streams of water, so my soul pants for
You, O God. My soul thirsts for God, for the living God.
Psalm 42:1-2

"I will not forget you! See, I have engraved
you on the palms of My hands."
Isaiah 49:15-16

Create in me a pure heart, O God,
and renew a steadfast spirit within me.
Psalm 51:10

"If you remain in Me and My words remain in you,
ask whatever you wish, and it will be given you."
John 15:7

Guide me in Your truth and teach me, for You are
God my Savior, and my hope is in You all day long.
Psalm 25:5

Praise God in His sanctuary; praise Him in His mighty
heavens. Praise Him for His acts of power; praise
Him for His surpassing greatness.
Psalm 150:1-2

He will keep you strong to the end, so that you will be
blameless on the day of our Lord Jesus Christ.
1 Corinthians 1:8

"Whoever comes to Me I will never drive away. For My Father's will is that everyone who looks to the Son and believes in Him shall have eternal life."

John 6:37, 40

You will keep in perfect peace him whose mind is steadfast,
because he trusts in You. Trust in the LORD forever, for
the LORD, the LORD, is the Rock eternal.
Isaiah 26:3-4

Praise and glory and wisdom and thanks and honor and power
and strength be to our God for ever and ever. Amen!
Revelation 7:12

May the God of hope fill you with all joy and peace
as you trust in Him, so that you may overflow with
hope by the power of the Holy Spirit.

Romans 15:13

Keep me as the apple of Your eye;
hide me in the shadow of Your wings.
Psalm 17:8

Delight yourself in the LORD and He will
give you the desires of your heart.
Psalm 37:4

"I will instruct you and teach you in the way you should go;
I will counsel you and watch over you."
Psalm 32.8

Commit to the LORD whatever you do,
and your plans will succeed.
Proverbs 16:3

Search me, O God, and know my heart; test me and know
my anxious thoughts. See if there is any offensive way
in me, and lead me in the way everlasting.
Psalm 139:23-24

The eternal God is your refuge,
and underneath are the everlasting arms.
Deuteronomy 33:27

Those who hope in the LORD will renew their strength. They will
soar on wings like eagles; they will run and not grow weary,
they will walk and not be faint.

Isaiah 40:31

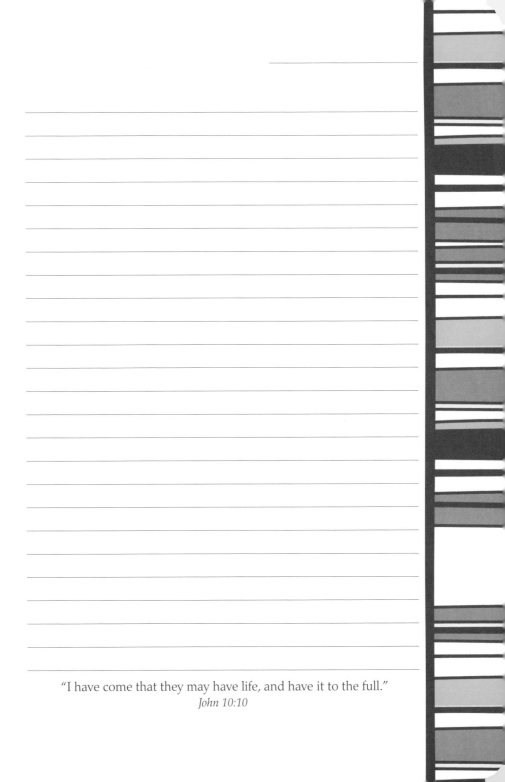

"I have come that they may have life, and have it to the full."
John 10:10

O LORD, You are my God; I will exalt You and praise Your name,
for in perfect faithfulness You have done marvelous things.
Isaiah 25:1

_____

_____

_____

_____

_____

_____

_____

_____

_____

_____

_____

_____

_____

_____

_____

_____

_____

_____

_____

_____

_____

_____

_____

_____

"I know the plans I have for you," declares the LORD, "plans to prosper
you and not to harm you, plans to give you hope and a future."
Jeremiah 29:11

Shout for joy, O heavens; rejoice, O earth; burst into song,
O mountains! For the LORD comforts His people.
Isaiah 49:13

"Peace I leave with you; My peace I give you. Do not let your
hearts be troubled and do not be afraid."
John 14:27

He who began a good work in you will carry it on
to completion until the day of Christ Jesus.
Philippians 1:6

We know that in all things God works for the good of those
who love Him, who have been called according to His purpose.
Romans 8:28

Blessed are those who walk in the light of Your presence,
O Lord. They rejoice in Your name all day long;
they exult in Your righteousness.
Psalm 89:15-16

God is able to make all grace abound to you, so that
in all things at all times, having all that you need,
you will abound in every good work.
2 Corinthians 9:8

"The Lord bless you and keep you; the Lord make His face
shine upon you and be gracious to you; the Lord turn
His face toward you and give you peace."
Numbers 6:24-26

God has said, "Never will I leave you; never will I forsake you."
Hebrews 13:5

Every good and perfect gift is from above, coming down from
the Father of the heavenly lights, who does not
change like shifting shadows.
James 1:17

May the God of peace equip you with everything good for doing
His will, through Jesus Christ, to whom be glory for ever and ever.
Hebrews 13:20-21

The LORD is good, a refuge in times of trouble.
He cares for those who trust in Him.
Nahum 1:7

As the deer pants for streams of water, so my soul pants for
You, O God. My soul thirsts for God, for the living God.
Psalm 42:1-2

"I will not forget you! See, I have engraved
you on the palms of My hands."
Isaiah 49:15-16

Create in me a pure heart, O God,
and renew a steadfast spirit within me.
Psalm 51:10

"If you remain in Me and My words remain in you,
ask whatever you wish, and it will be given you."
John 15:7

Guide me in Your truth and teach me, for You are
God my Savior, and my hope is in You all day long.
Psalm 25:5

Praise God in His sanctuary; praise Him in His mighty
heavens. Praise Him for His acts of power; praise
Him for His surpassing greatness.
Psalm 150:1-2

He will keep you strong to the end, so that you will be
blameless on the day of our Lord Jesus Christ.
1 Corinthians 1:8

"Whoever comes to Me I will never drive away. For My Father's will is that everyone who looks to the Son and believes in Him shall have eternal life."

John 6:37, 40

You will keep in perfect peace him whose mind is steadfast,
because he trusts in You. Trust in the LORD forever, for
the LORD, the LORD, is the Rock eternal.
Isaiah 26:3-4

Praise and glory and wisdom and thanks and honor and power
and strength be to our God for ever and ever. Amen!
Revelation 7:12

May the God of hope fill you with all joy and peace
as you trust in Him, so that you may overflow with
hope by the power of the Holy Spirit.
Romans 15:13

Keep me as the apple of Your eye;
hide me in the shadow of Your wings.
Psalm 17:8

Delight yourself in the LORD and He will
give you the desires of your heart.
Psalm 37:4

_____

"I will instruct you and teach you in the way you should go;
I will counsel you and watch over you."
Psalm 32:8

Commit to the LORD whatever you do,
and your plans will succeed.
Proverbs 16:3

Search me, O God, and know my heart; test me and know
my anxious thoughts. See if there is any offensive way
in me, and lead me in the way everlasting.
Psalm 139:23-24

The eternal God is your refuge,
and underneath are the everlasting arms.
Deuteronomy 33:27

Those who hope in the LORD will renew their strength. They will
soar on wings like eagles; they will run and not grow weary,
they will walk and not be faint.

Isaiah 40:31

"I have come that they may have life, and have it to the full."
John 10:10

O LORD, You are my God; I will exalt You and praise Your name,
for in perfect faithfulness You have done marvelous things.
Isaiah 25:1

"I know the plans I have for you," declares the LORD, "plans to prosper you and not to harm you, plans to give you hope and a future."
Jeremiah 29:11

Shout for joy, O heavens; rejoice, O earth; burst into song,
O mountains! For the LORD comforts His people.
Isaiah 49:13

_____

_____
_____
_____
_____
_____
_____
_____
_____
_____
_____
_____
_____
_____
_____
_____
_____
_____
_____
_____
_____
_____
_____
_____
_____
_____

"Peace I leave with you; My peace I give you. Do not let your
hearts be troubled and do not be afraid."
John 14:27

He who began a good work in you will carry it on
to completion until the day of Christ Jesus.
Philippians 1:6

We know that in all things God works for the good of those
who love Him, who have been called according to His purpose.
Romans 8:28

Blessed are those who walk in the light of Your presence,
O Lord. They rejoice in Your name all day long;
they exult in Your righteousness.
Psalm 89:15-16

God is able to make all grace abound to you, so that
in all things at all times, having all that you need,
you will abound in every good work.
2 Corinthians 9:8

"The LORD bless you and keep you; the LORD make His face
shine upon you and be gracious to you; the LORD turn
His face toward you and give you peace."
Numbers 6:24-26

God has said, "Never will I leave you; never will I forsake you."
Hebrews 13:5

Every good and perfect gift is from above, coming down from
the Father of the heavenly lights, who does not
change like shifting shadows.
James 1:17

May the God of peace equip you with everything good for doing
His will, through Jesus Christ, to whom be glory for ever and ever.
Hebrews 13:20-21

The LORD is good, a refuge in times of trouble.
He cares for those who trust in Him.
Nahum 1:7

As the deer pants for streams of water, so my soul pants for
You, O God. My soul thirsts for God, for the living God.
Psalm 42:1-2

"I will not forget you! See, I have engraved
you on the palms of My hands."
Isaiah 49:15-16

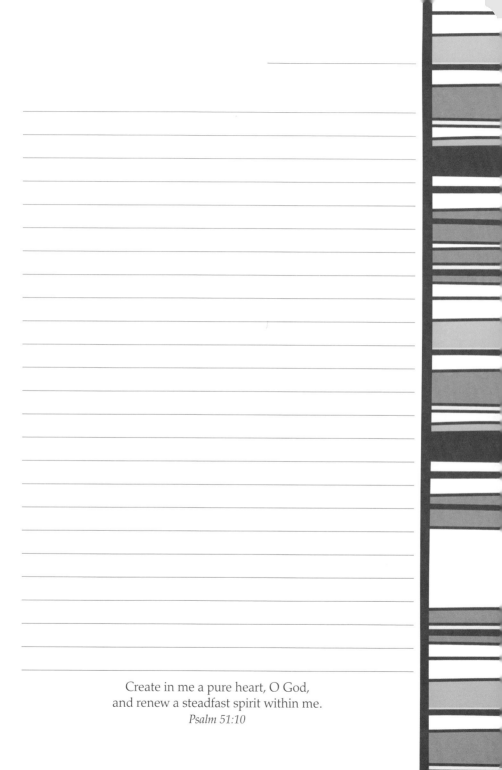

Create in me a pure heart, O God,
and renew a steadfast spirit within me.
Psalm 51:10

"If you remain in Me and My words remain in you,
ask whatever you wish, and it will be given you."
John 15:7

Guide me in Your truth and teach me, for You are
God my Savior, and my hope is in You all day long.
Psalm 25:5

Praise God in His sanctuary; praise Him in His mighty
heavens. Praise Him for His acts of power; praise
Him for His surpassing greatness.
Psalm 150:1-2

He will keep you strong to the end, so that you will be
blameless on the day of our Lord Jesus Christ.
1 Corinthians 1:8

"Whoever comes to Me I will never drive away. For My Father's will is that everyone who looks to the Son and believes in Him shall have eternal life."

John 6:37, 40

You will keep in perfect peace him whose mind is steadfast,
because he trusts in You. Trust in the LORD forever, for
the LORD, the LORD, is the Rock eternal.

Isaiah 26:3-4

Praise and glory and wisdom and thanks and honor and power
and strength be to our God for ever and ever. Amen!
Revelation 7:12

May the God of hope fill you with all joy and peace
as you trust in Him, so that you may overflow with
hope by the power of the Holy Spirit.

Romans 15:13

Keep me as the apple of Your eye;
hide me in the shadow of Your wings.

Psalm 17:8

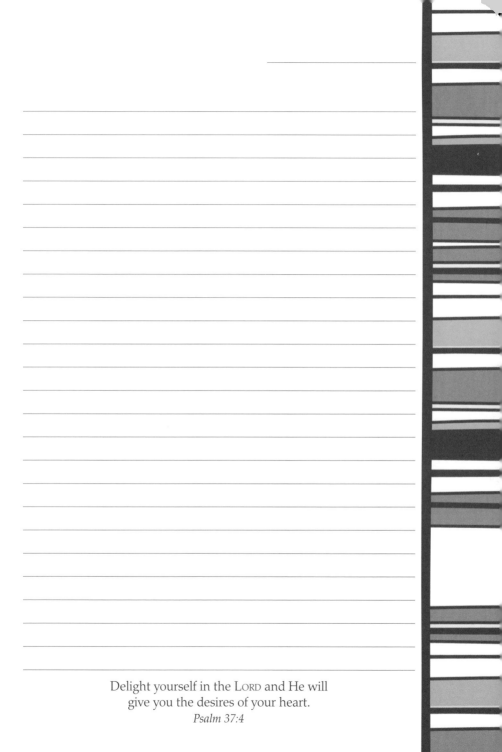

Delight yourself in the Lord and He will
give you the desires of your heart.
Psalm 37:4

"I will instruct you and teach you in the way you should go;
I will counsel you and watch over you."
Psalm 32:8

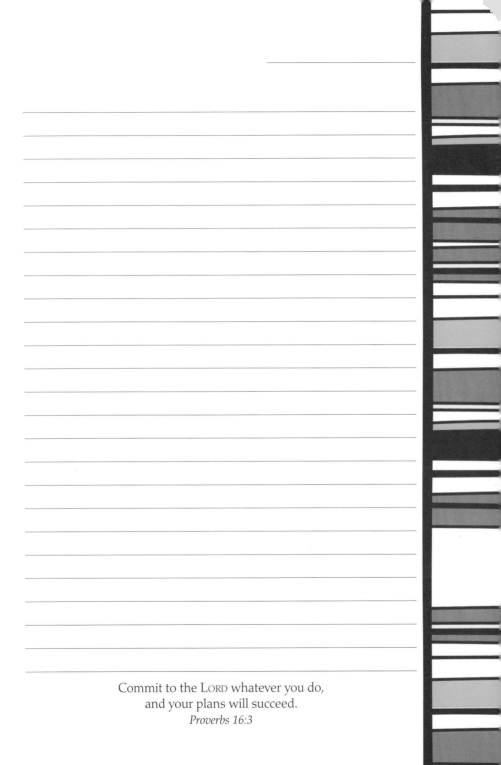

Commit to the LORD whatever you do,
and your plans will succeed.
Proverbs 16:3

Search me, O God, and know my heart; test me and know
my anxious thoughts. See if there is any offensive way
in me, and lead me in the way everlasting.
Psalm 139:23-24

The eternal God is your refuge,
and underneath are the everlasting arms.
Deuteronomy 33:27

Those who hope in the Lord will renew their strength. They will
soar on wings like eagles; they will run and not grow weary,
they will walk and not be faint.

Isaiah 40:31

"I have come that they may have life, and have it to the full."
John 10:10

_____

O LORD, You are my God; I will exalt You and praise Your name,
for in perfect faithfulness You have done marvelous things.
Isaiah 25:1

"I know the plans I have for you," declares the LORD, "plans to prosper you and not to harm you, plans to give you hope and a future."
Jeremiah 29:11

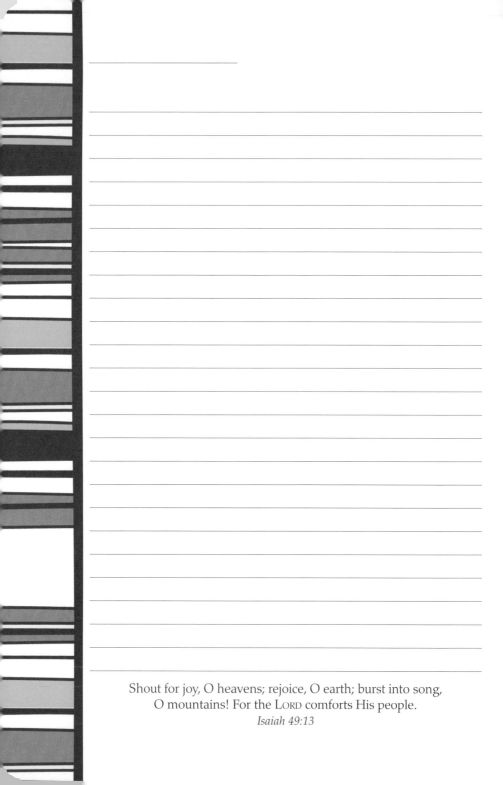

Shout for joy, O heavens; rejoice, O earth; burst into song,
O mountains! For the LORD comforts His people.
Isaiah 49:13

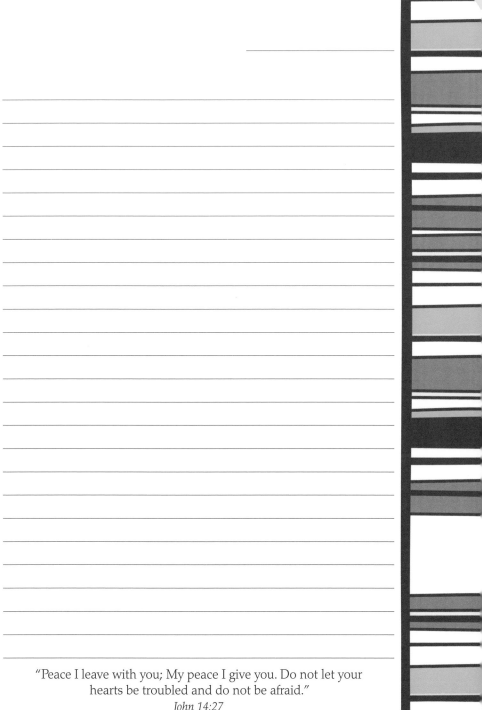

"Peace I leave with you; My peace I give you. Do not let your
hearts be troubled and do not be afraid."

John 14:27

He who began a good work in you will carry it on
to completion until the day of Christ Jesus.
Philippians 1:6

We know that in all things God works for the good of those
who love Him, who have been called according to His purpose.
Romans 8:28

Blessed are those who walk in the light of Your presence,
O Lord. They rejoice in Your name all day long;
they exult in Your righteousness.
Psalm 89:15-16

God is able to make all grace abound to you, so that
in all things at all times, having all that you need,
you will abound in every good work.
2 Corinthians 9:8

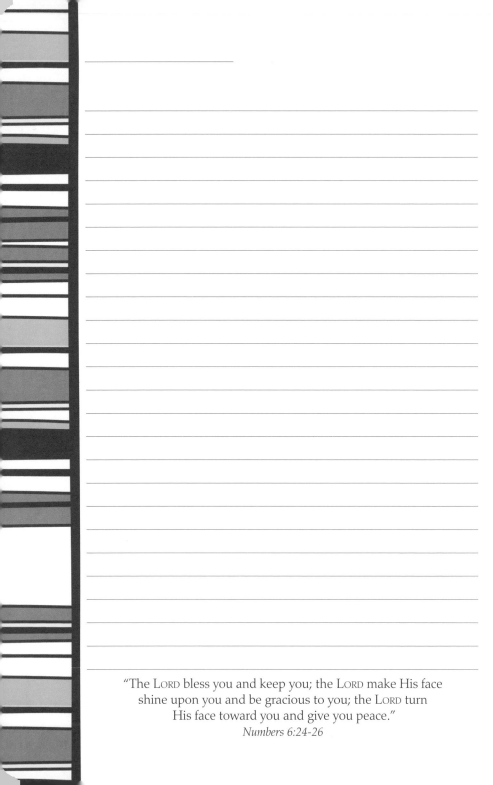

"The LORD bless you and keep you; the LORD make His face
shine upon you and be gracious to you; the LORD turn
His face toward you and give you peace."
Numbers 6:24-26

God has said, "Never will I leave you; never will I forsake you."
Hebrews 13:5

Every good and perfect gift is from above, coming down from
the Father of the heavenly lights, who does not
change like shifting shadows.

James 1:17

May the God of peace equip you with everything good for doing
His will, through Jesus Christ, to whom be glory for ever and ever.
Hebrews 13:20-21

The Lord is good, a refuge in times of trouble.
He cares for those who trust in Him.
Nahum 1:7

As the deer pants for streams of water, so my soul pants for
You, O God. My soul thirsts for God, for the living God.
Psalm 42:1-2

"I will not forget you! See, I have engraved
you on the palms of My hands."
Isaiah 49:15-16

Create in me a pure heart, O God,
and renew a steadfast spirit within me.
Psalm 51:10

_____

"If you remain in Me and My words remain in you,
ask whatever you wish, and it will be given you."
John 15:7

Guide me in Your truth and teach me, for You are
God my Savior, and my hope is in You all day long.
Psalm 25:5

Praise God in His sanctuary; praise Him in His mighty
heavens. Praise Him for His acts of power; praise
Him for His surpassing greatness.
Psalm 150:1-2

He will keep you strong to the end, so that you will be
blameless on the day of our Lord Jesus Christ.
1 Corinthians 1:8

"Whoever comes to Me I will never drive away. For My Father's will is that everyone who looks to the Son and believes in Him shall have eternal life."

John 6:37, 40

You will keep in perfect peace him whose mind is steadfast,
because he trusts in You. Trust in the LORD forever, for
the LORD, the LORD, is the Rock eternal.
Isaiah 26:3-4

Praise and glory and wisdom and thanks and honor and power
and strength be to our God for ever and ever. Amen!
Revelation 7:12

May the God of hope fill you with all joy and peace
as you trust in Him, so that you may overflow with
hope by the power of the Holy Spirit.

Romans 15:13

Keep me as the apple of Your eye;
hide me in the shadow of Your wings.
Psalm 17:8

Delight yourself in the LORD and He will
give you the desires of your heart.
Psalm 37:4

"I will instruct you and teach you in the way you should go;
I will counsel you and watch over you."
Psalm 32:8

Commit to the LORD whatever you do,
and your plans will succeed.
Proverbs 16:3

Search me, O God, and know my heart; test me and know
my anxious thoughts. See if there is any offensive way
in me, and lead me in the way everlasting.
Psalm 139:23-24

The eternal God is your refuge,
and underneath are the everlasting arms.
Deuteronomy 33:27

Those who hope in the LORD will renew their strength. They will
soar on wings like eagles; they will run and not grow weary,
they will walk and not be faint.

Isaiah 40:31

"I have come that they may have life, and have it to the full."
John 10:10

O LORD, You are my God; I will exalt You and praise Your name,
for in perfect faithfulness You have done marvelous things.
Isaiah 25:1

"I know the plans I have for you," declares the LORD, "plans to prosper you and not to harm you, plans to give you hope and a future."
Jeremiah 29:11

Shout for joy, O heavens; rejoice, O earth; burst into song,
O mountains! For the LORD comforts His people.

Isaiah 49:13

"Peace I leave with you; My peace I give you. Do not let your hearts be troubled and do not be afraid."
John 14:27

He who began a good work in you will carry it on
to completion until the day of Christ Jesus.
Philippians 1:6

We know that in all things God works for the good of those
who love Him, who have been called according to His purpose.
Romans 8:28

Blessed are those who walk in the light of Your presence,
O LORD. They rejoice in Your name all day long;
they exult in Your righteousness.

Psalm 89:15-16

God is able to make all grace abound to you, so that
in all things at all times, having all that you need,
you will abound in every good work.
2 Corinthians 9:8

"The LORD bless you and keep you; the LORD make His face
shine upon you and be gracious to you; the LORD turn
His face toward you and give you peace."
Numbers 6:24-26

God has said, "Never will I leave you; never will I forsake you."
Hebrews 13:5

Every good and perfect gift is from above, coming down from
the Father of the heavenly lights, who does not
change like shifting shadows.
James 1:17

May the God of peace equip you with everything good for doing
His will, through Jesus Christ, to whom be glory for ever and ever.
Hebrews 13:20-21

The Lord is good, a refuge in times of trouble.
He cares for those who trust in Him.
Nahum 1:7

As the deer pants for streams of water, so my soul pants for
You, O God. My soul thirsts for God, for the living God.
Psalm 42:1-2

"I will not forget you! See, I have engraved
you on the palms of My hands."
Isaiah 49:15-16

Create in me a pure heart, O God,
and renew a steadfast spirit within me.
Psalm 51:10

"If you remain in Me and My words remain in you,
ask whatever you wish, and it will be given you."
John 15:7

Guide me in Your truth and teach me, for You are
God my Savior, and my hope is in You all day long.
Psalm 25:5

Praise God in His sanctuary; praise Him in His mighty
heavens. Praise Him for His acts of power; praise
Him for His surpassing greatness.
Psalm 150:1-2

He will keep you strong to the end, so that you will be
blameless on the day of our Lord Jesus Christ.

1 Corinthians 1:8

"Whoever comes to Me I will never drive away. For My Father's will is that everyone who looks to the Son and believes in Him shall have eternal life."
John 6:37, 40

You will keep in perfect peace him whose mind is steadfast,
because he trusts in You. Trust in the LORD forever, for
the LORD, the LORD, is the Rock eternal.

Isaiah 26:3-4

Praise and glory and wisdom and thanks and honor and power
and strength be to our God for ever and ever. Amen!
Revelation 7:12

May the God of hope fill you with all joy and peace
as you trust in Him, so that you may overflow with
hope by the power of the Holy Spirit.
Romans 15:13

Keep me as the apple of Your eye;
hide me in the shadow of Your wings.
Psalm 17:8

Delight yourself in the Lᴏʀᴅ and He will
give you the desires of your heart.
Psalm 37:4

"I will instruct you and teach you in the way you should go;
I will counsel you and watch over you."
Psalm 32:8

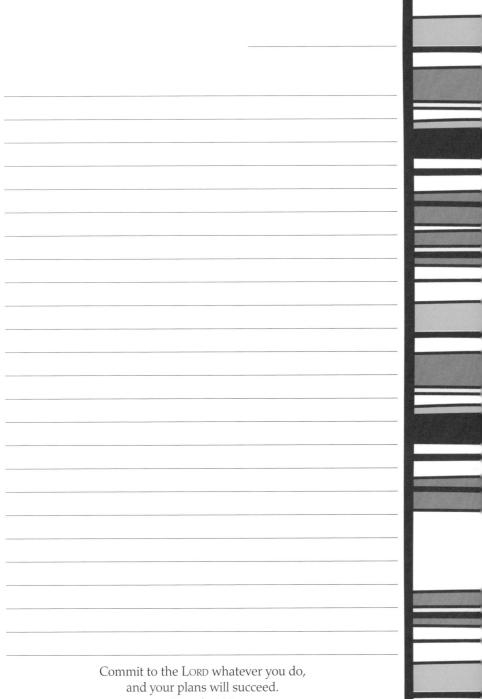

Commit to the LORD whatever you do,
and your plans will succeed.
Proverbs 16:3

Search me, O God, and know my heart; test me and know
my anxious thoughts. See if there is any offensive way
in me, and lead me in the way everlasting.
Psalm 139:23-24

The eternal God is your refuge,
and underneath are the everlasting arms.
Deuteronomy 33:27

Those who hope in the LORD will renew their strength. They will
soar on wings like eagles; they will run and not grow weary,
they will walk and not be faint.

Isaiah 40:31

"I have come that they may have life, and have it to the full."
John 10:10

O Lᴏʀᴅ, You are my God; I will exalt You and praise Your name,
for in perfect faithfulness You have done marvelous things.
Isaiah 25:1

"I know the plans I have for you," declares the LORD, "plans to prosper
you and not to harm you, plans to give you hope and a future."
Jeremiah 29:11

Shout for joy, O heavens; rejoice, O earth; burst into song,
O mountains! For the LORD comforts His people.

Isaiah 49:13

"Peace I leave with you; My peace I give you. Do not let your
hearts be troubled and do not be afraid."
John 14:27

He who began a good work in you will carry it on
to completion until the day of Christ Jesus.
Philippians 1:6

We know that in all things God works for the good of those
who love Him, who have been called according to His purpose.

Romans 8:28

Blessed are those who walk in the light of Your presence,
O Lord. They rejoice in Your name all day long;
they exult in Your righteousness.
Psalm 89:15-16

God is able to make all grace abound to you, so that
in all things at all times, having all that you need,
you will abound in every good work.
2 Corinthians 9:8

"The Lord bless you and keep you; the Lord make His face
shine upon you and be gracious to you; the Lord turn
His face toward you and give you peace."
Numbers 6:24-26

God has said, "Never will I leave you; never will I forsake you."
Hebrews 13:5

Every good and perfect gift is from above, coming down from
the Father of the heavenly lights, who does not
change like shifting shadows.
James 1:17

May the God of peace equip you with everything good for doing
His will, through Jesus Christ, to whom be glory for ever and ever.
Hebrews 13:20-21

The LORD is good, a refuge in times of trouble.
He cares for those who trust in Him.
Nahum 1:7

As the deer pants for streams of water, so my soul pants for
You, O God. My soul thirsts for God, for the living God.
Psalm 42:1-2

"I will not forget you! See, I have engraved
you on the palms of My hands."
Isaiah 49:15-16

Create in me a pure heart, O God,
and renew a steadfast spirit within me.
Psalm 51:10

"If you remain in Me and My words remain in you,
ask whatever you wish, and it will be given you."
John 15:7

Guide me in Your truth and teach me, for You are
God my Savior, and my hope is in You all day long.

Psalm 25:5

Praise God in His sanctuary; praise Him in His mighty
heavens. Praise Him for His acts of power; praise
Him for His surpassing greatness.
Psalm 150:1-2

He will keep you strong to the end, so that you will be
blameless on the day of our Lord Jesus Christ.
1 Corinthians 1:8

"Whoever comes to Me I will never drive away. For My Father's will is that everyone who looks to the Son and believes in Him shall have eternal life."

John 6:37, 40

You will keep in perfect peace him whose mind is steadfast,
because he trusts in You. Trust in the LORD forever, for
the LORD, the LORD, is the Rock eternal.

Isaiah 26:3-4

Praise and glory and wisdom and thanks and honor and power
and strength be to our God for ever and ever. Amen!
Revelation 7:12

May the God of hope fill you with all joy and peace
as you trust in Him, so that you may overflow with
hope by the power of the Holy Spirit.

Romans 15:13

Keep me as the apple of Your eye;
hide me in the shadow of Your wings.
Psalm 17:8

Delight yourself in the LORD and He will
give you the desires of your heart.
Psalm 37:4

_____

"I will instruct you and teach you in the way you should go;
I will counsel you and watch over you."
Psalm 32:8

Commit to the LORD whatever you do,
and your plans will succeed.
Proverbs 16:3

Search me, O God, and know my heart; test me and know
my anxious thoughts. See if there is any offensive way
in me, and lead me in the way everlasting.
Psalm 139:23-24

The eternal God is your refuge,
and underneath are the everlasting arms.
Deuteronomy 33:27

Those who hope in the LORD will renew their strength. They will
soar on wings like eagles; they will run and not grow weary,
they will walk and not be faint.

Isaiah 40:31

"I have come that they may have life, and have it to the full."
John 10:10

O Lord, You are my God; I will exalt You and praise Your name,
for in perfect faithfulness You have done marvelous things.
Isaiah 25:1

_____

"I know the plans I have for you," declares the LORD, "plans to prosper you and not to harm you, plans to give you hope and a future."
Jeremiah 29:11

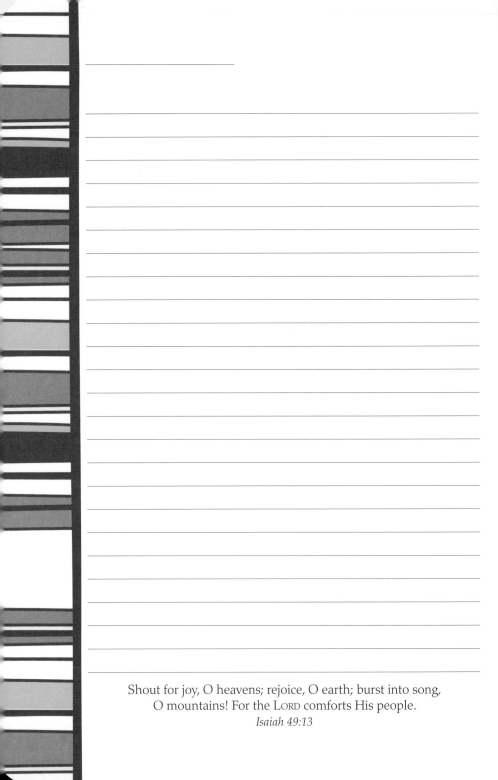

Shout for joy, O heavens; rejoice, O earth; burst into song,
O mountains! For the LORD comforts His people.
Isaiah 49:13

"Peace I leave with you; My peace I give you. Do not let your hearts be troubled and do not be afraid."

John 14:27

He who began a good work in you will carry it on
to completion until the day of Christ Jesus.
Philippians 1:6

We know that in all things God works for the good of those
who love Him, who have been called according to His purpose.
Romans 8:28

Blessed are those who walk in the light of Your presence,
O LORD. They rejoice in Your name all day long;
they exult in Your righteousness.
Psalm 89:15-16

God is able to make all grace abound to you, so that
in all things at all times, having all that you need,
you will abound in every good work.

2 Corinthians 9:8

"The Lord bless you and keep you; the Lord make His face
shine upon you and be gracious to you; the Lord turn
His face toward you and give you peace."
Numbers 6:24-26

God has said, "Never will I leave you; never will I forsake you."
Hebrews 13:5

_____

Every good and perfect gift is from above, coming down from
the Father of the heavenly lights, who does not
change like shifting shadows.
James 1:17

May the God of peace equip you with everything good for doing
His will, through Jesus Christ, to whom be glory for ever and ever.
Hebrews 13:20-21

The LORD is good, a refuge in times of trouble.
He cares for those who trust in Him.
Nahum 1:7

As the deer pants for streams of water, so my soul pants for
You, O God. My soul thirsts for God, for the living God.
Psalm 42:1-2

"I will not forget you! See, I have engraved
you on the palms of My hands."
Isaiah 49:15-16

Create in me a pure heart, O God,
and renew a steadfast spirit within me.
Psalm 51:10

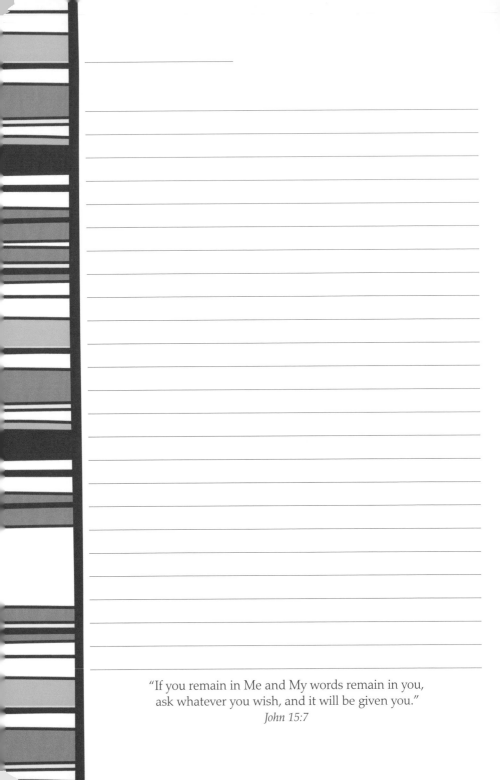

"If you remain in Me and My words remain in you,
ask whatever you wish, and it will be given you."
John 15:7

Guide me in Your truth and teach me, for You are
God my Savior, and my hope is in You all day long.
Psalm 25:5

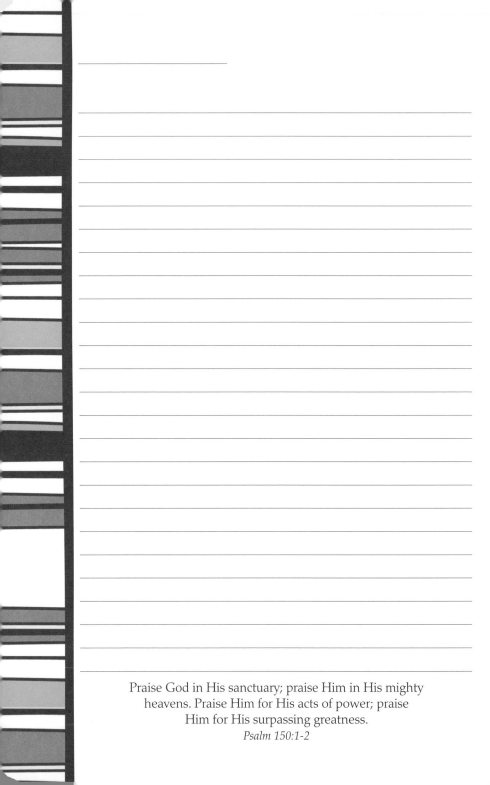

Praise God in His sanctuary; praise Him in His mighty
heavens. Praise Him for His acts of power; praise
Him for His surpassing greatness.
Psalm 150:1-2

He will keep you strong to the end, so that you will be
blameless on the day of our Lord Jesus Christ.
1 Corinthians 1:8

"Whoever comes to Me I will never drive away. For My
Father's will is that everyone who looks to the Son and
believes in Him shall have eternal life."
John 6:37, 40

You will keep in perfect peace him whose mind is steadfast,
because he trusts in You. Trust in the LORD forever, for
the LORD, the LORD, is the Rock eternal.
Isaiah 26:3-4

Praise and glory and wisdom and thanks and honor and power
and strength be to our God for ever and ever. Amen!
Revelation 7:12

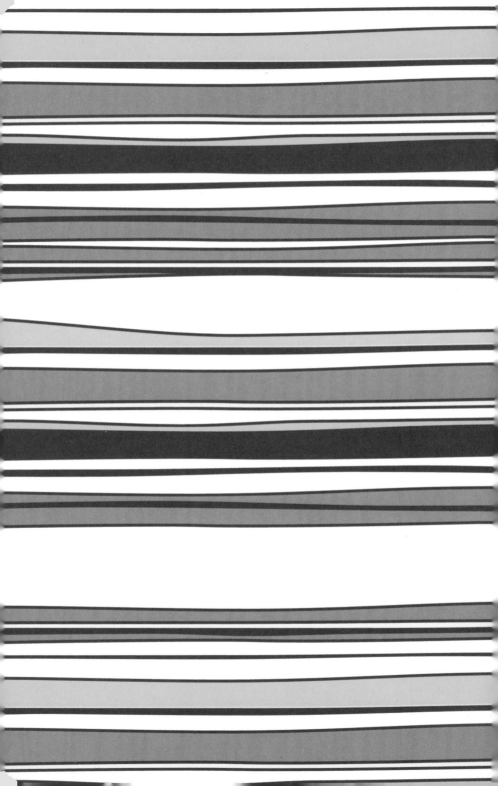